HALLOWEEN Memory BOOK

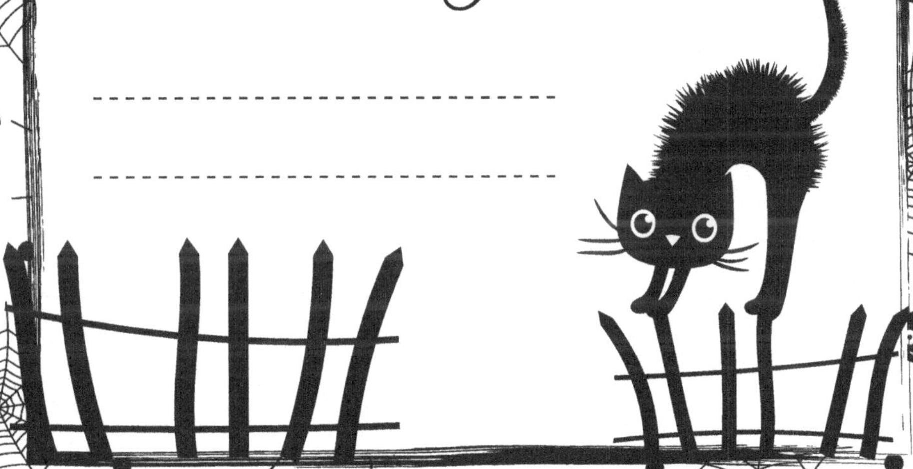

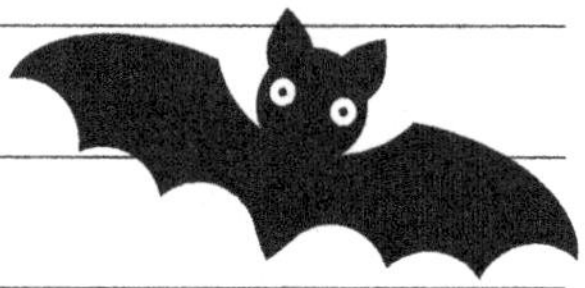

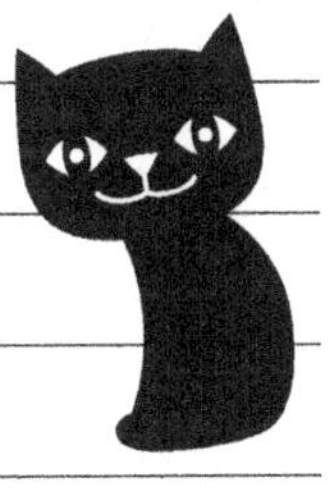

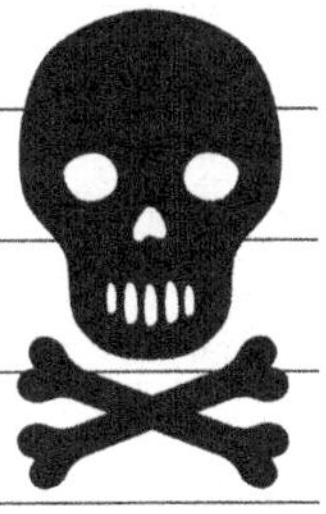

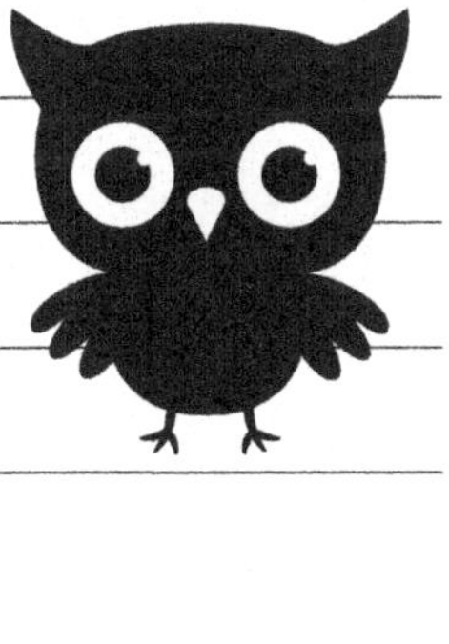

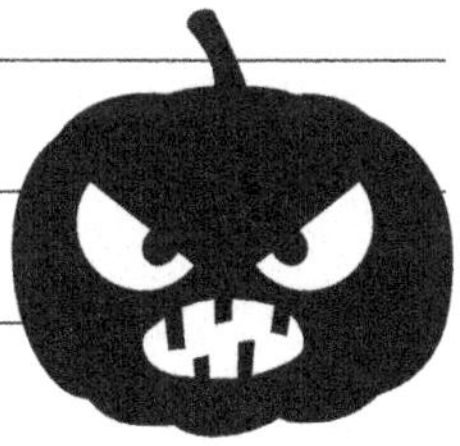

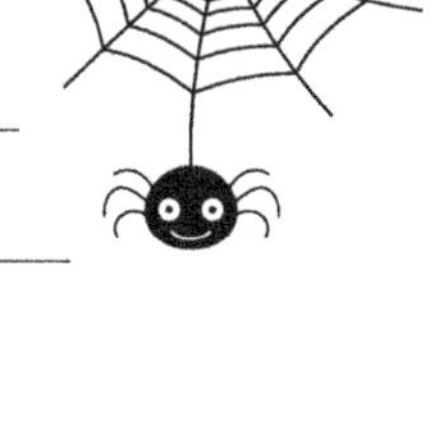

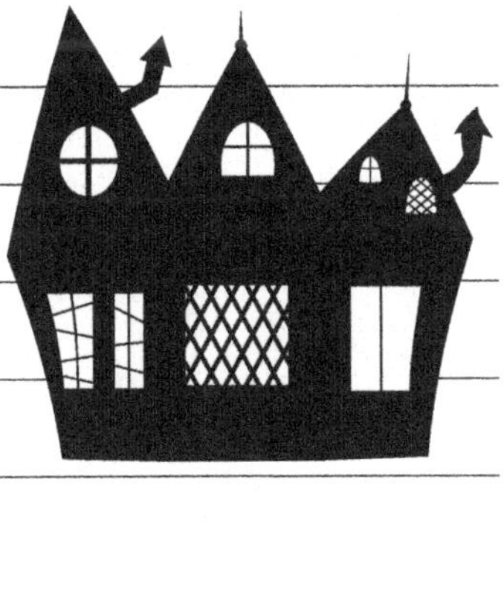

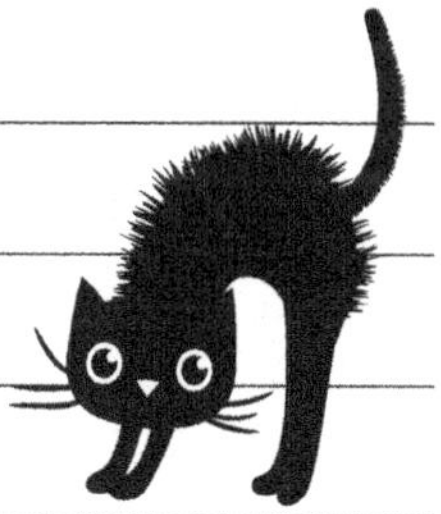

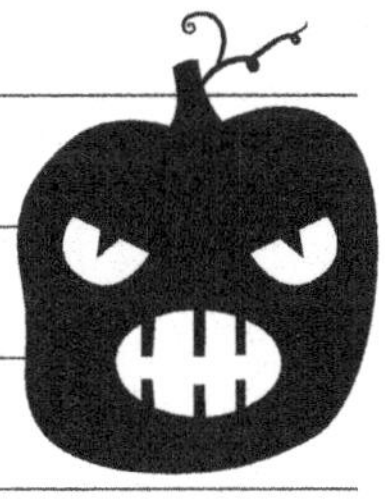

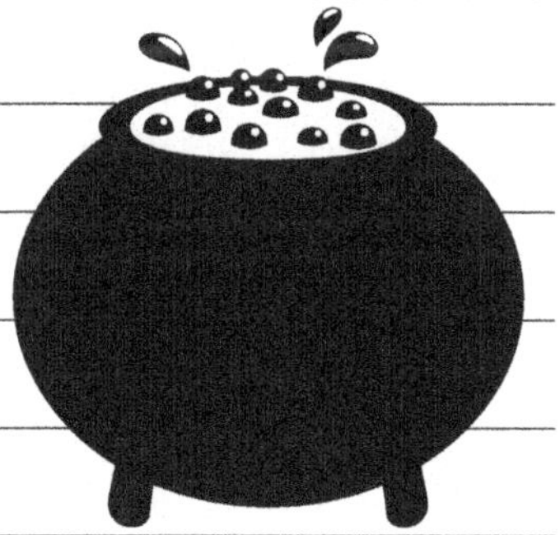

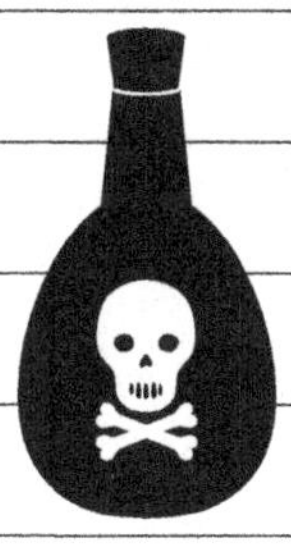

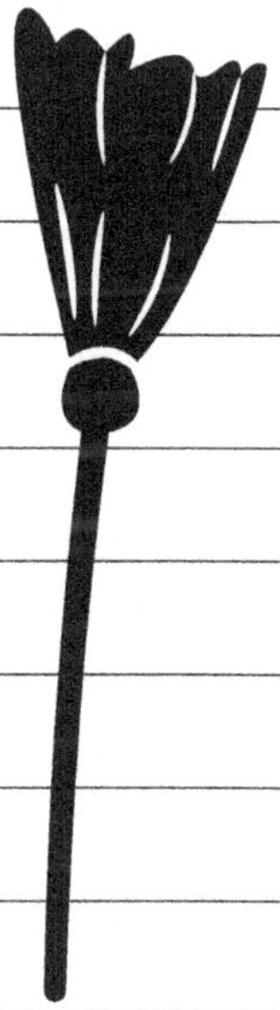

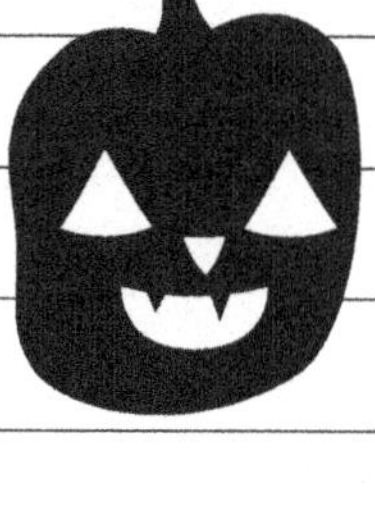

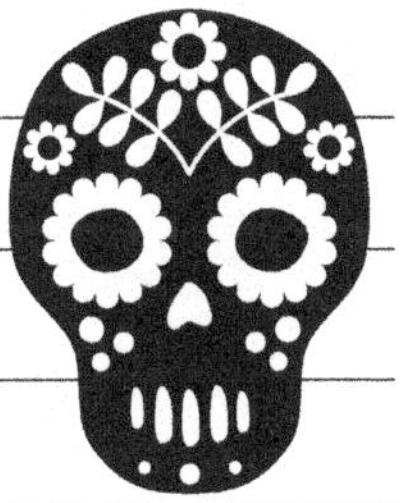

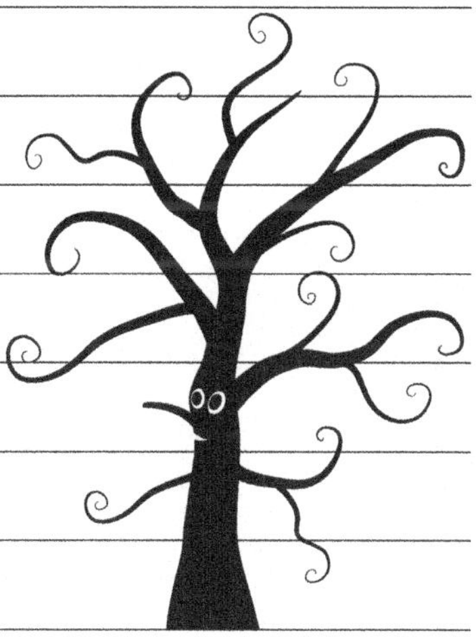

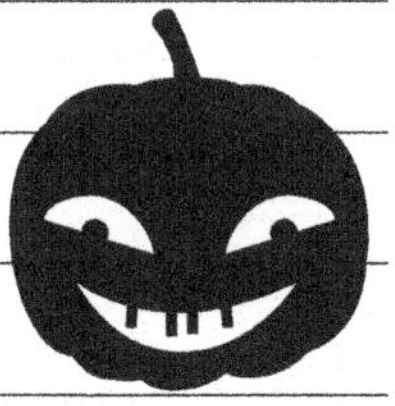

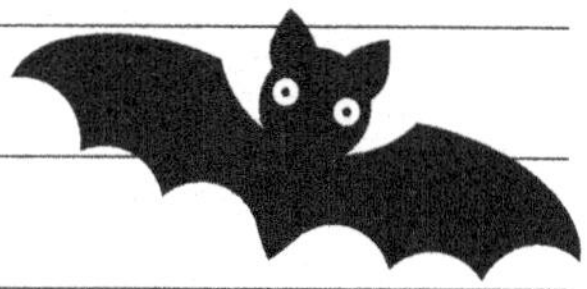

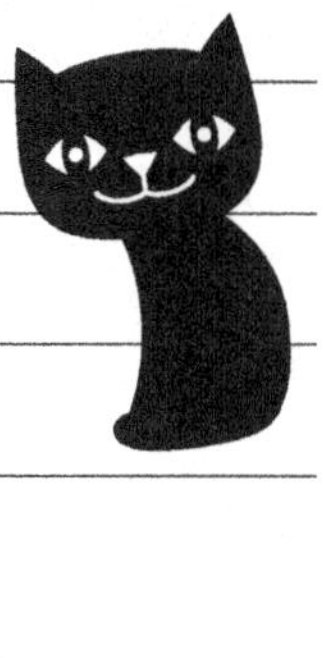

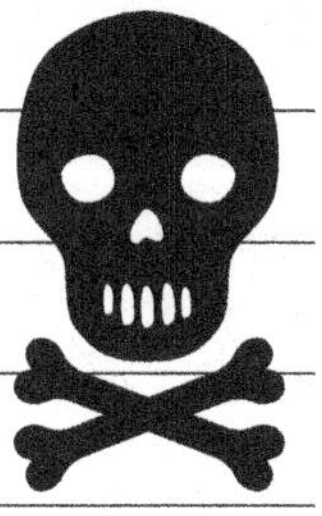

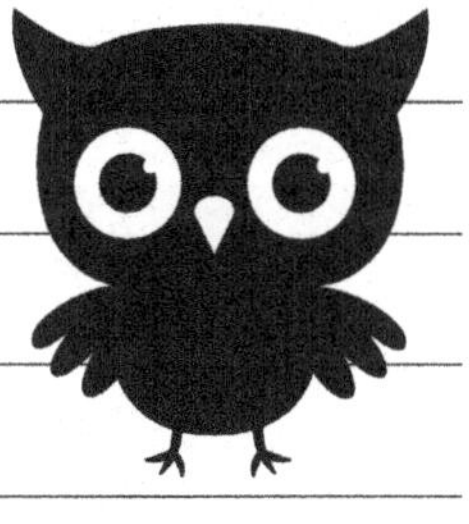

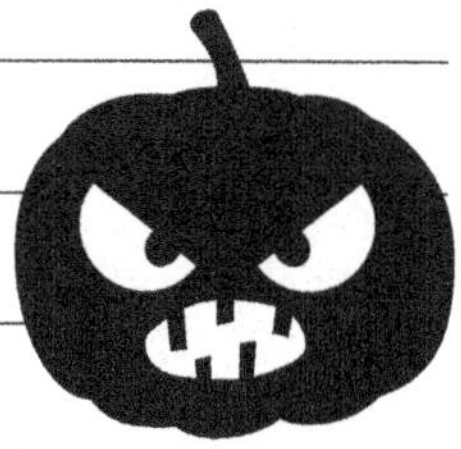

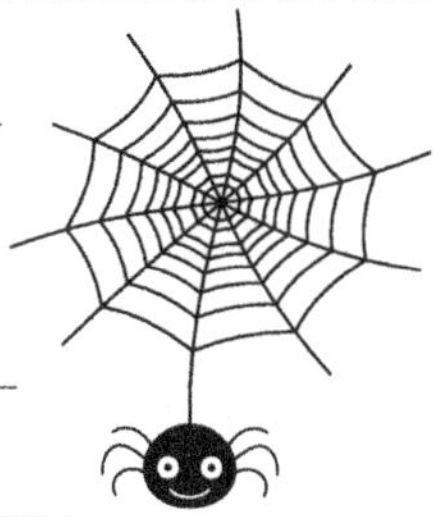

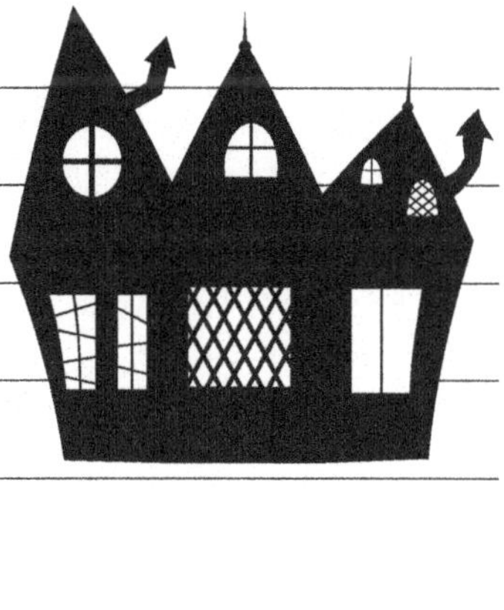

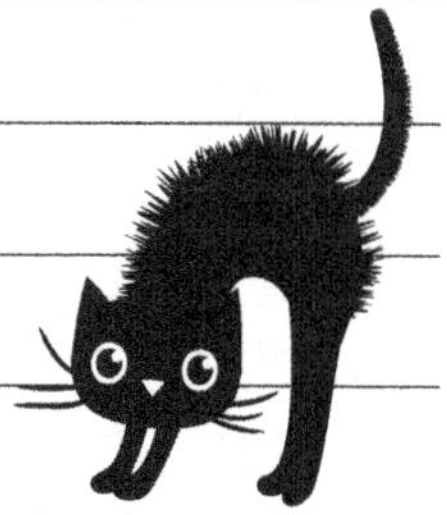

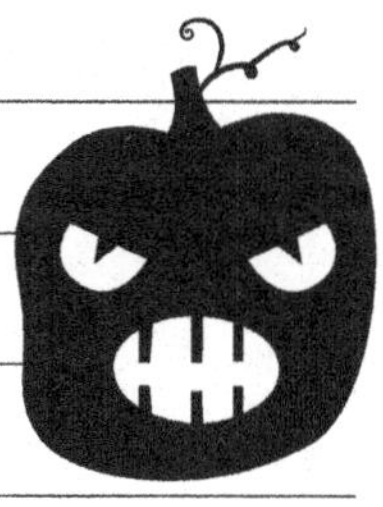

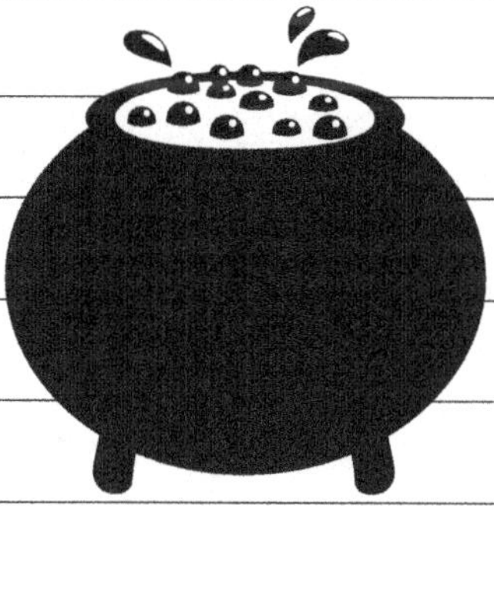

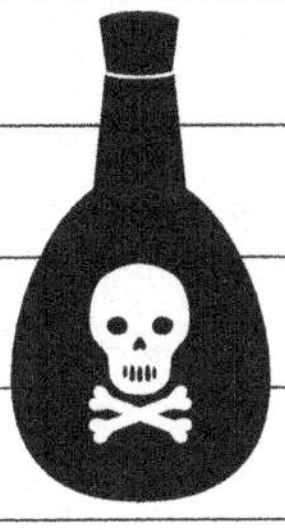

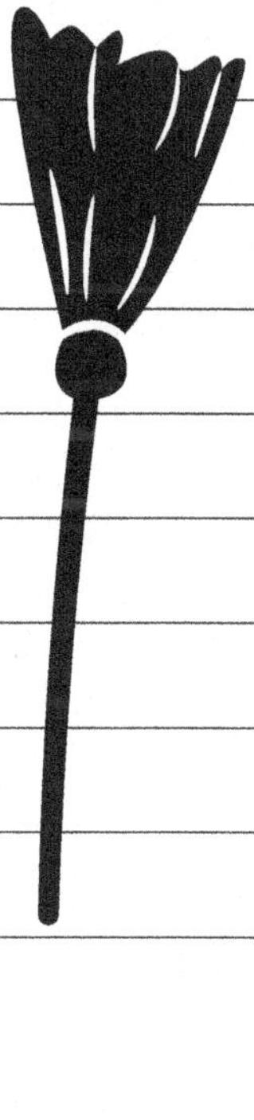

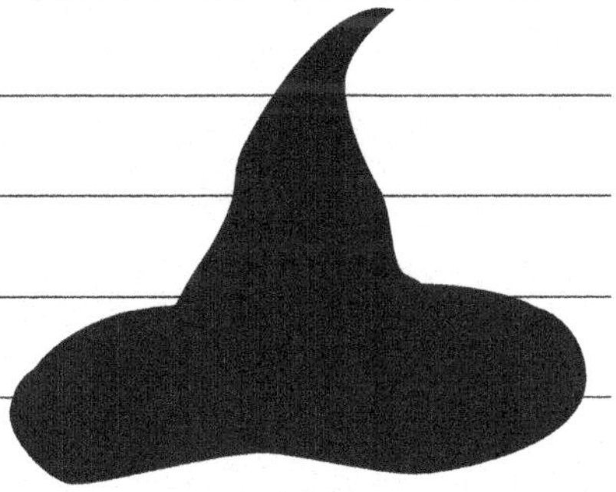

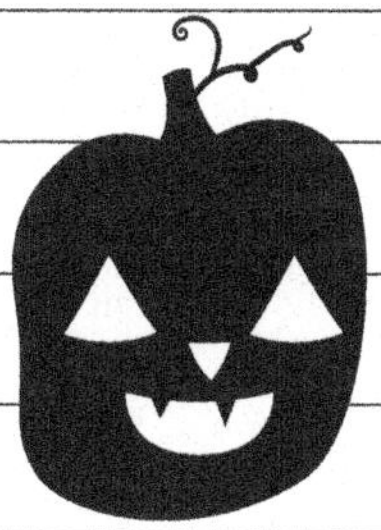

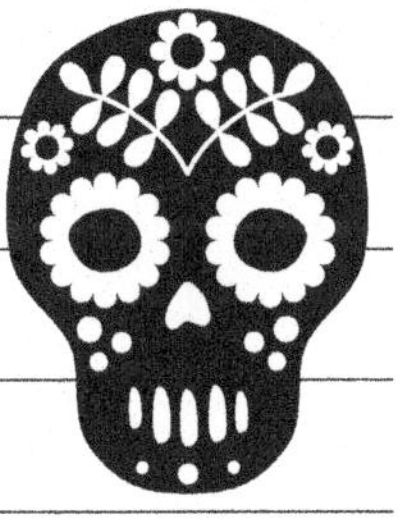

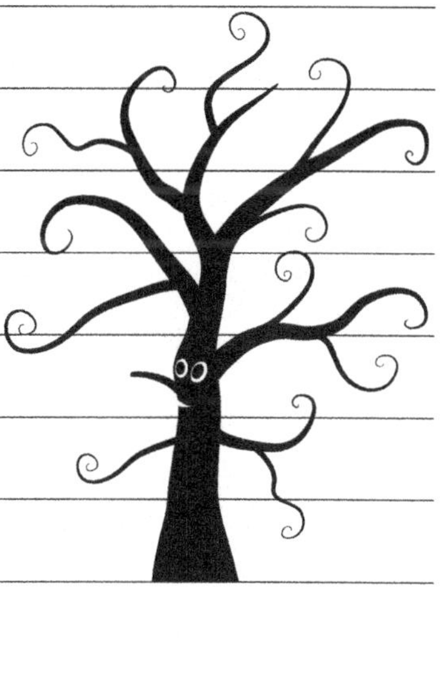

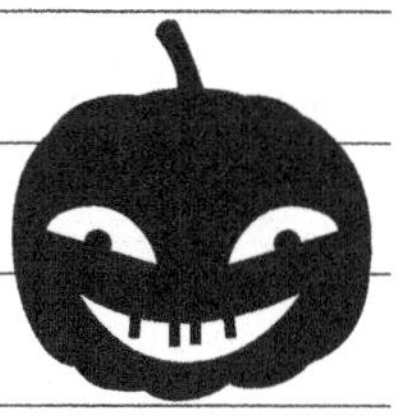

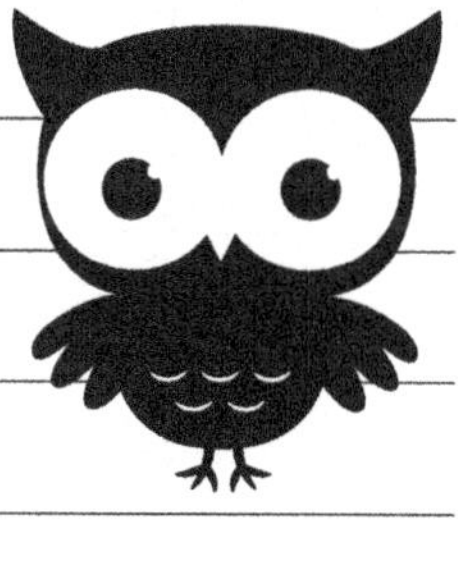

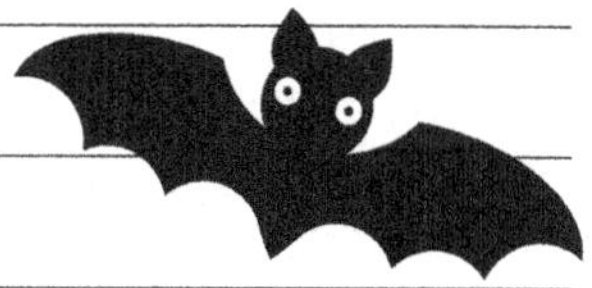

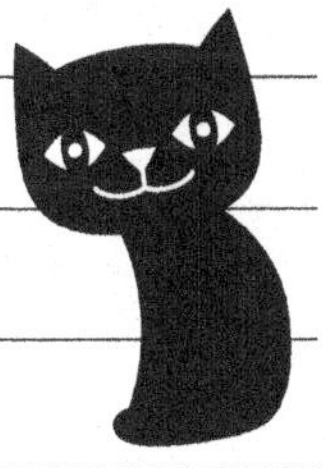

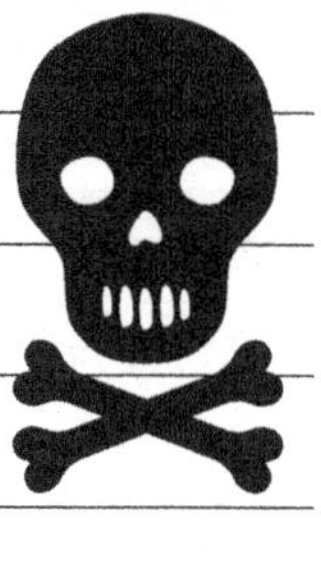

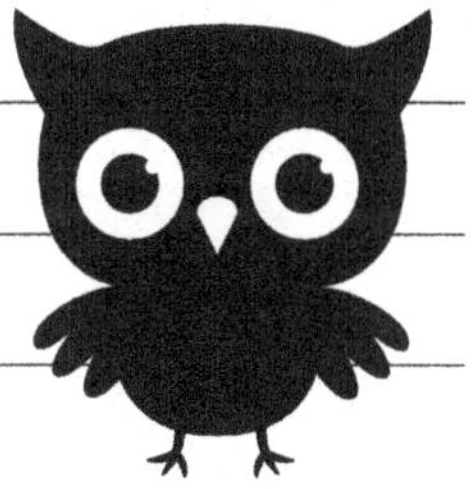

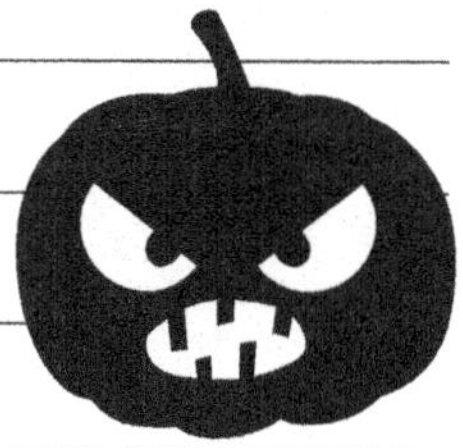

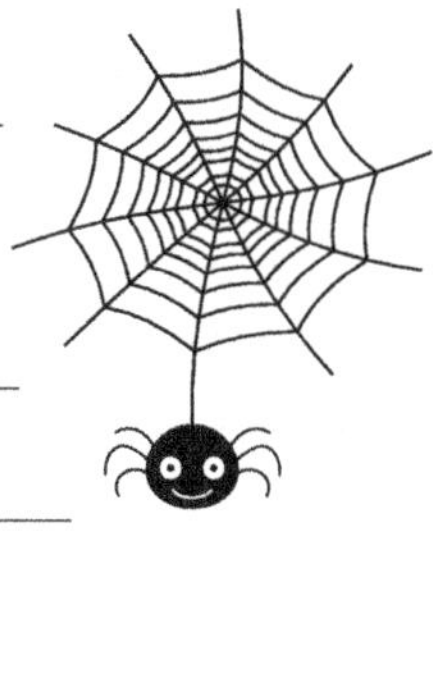

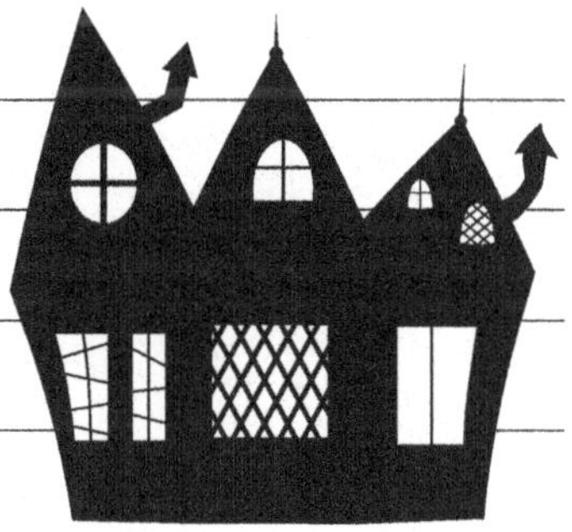

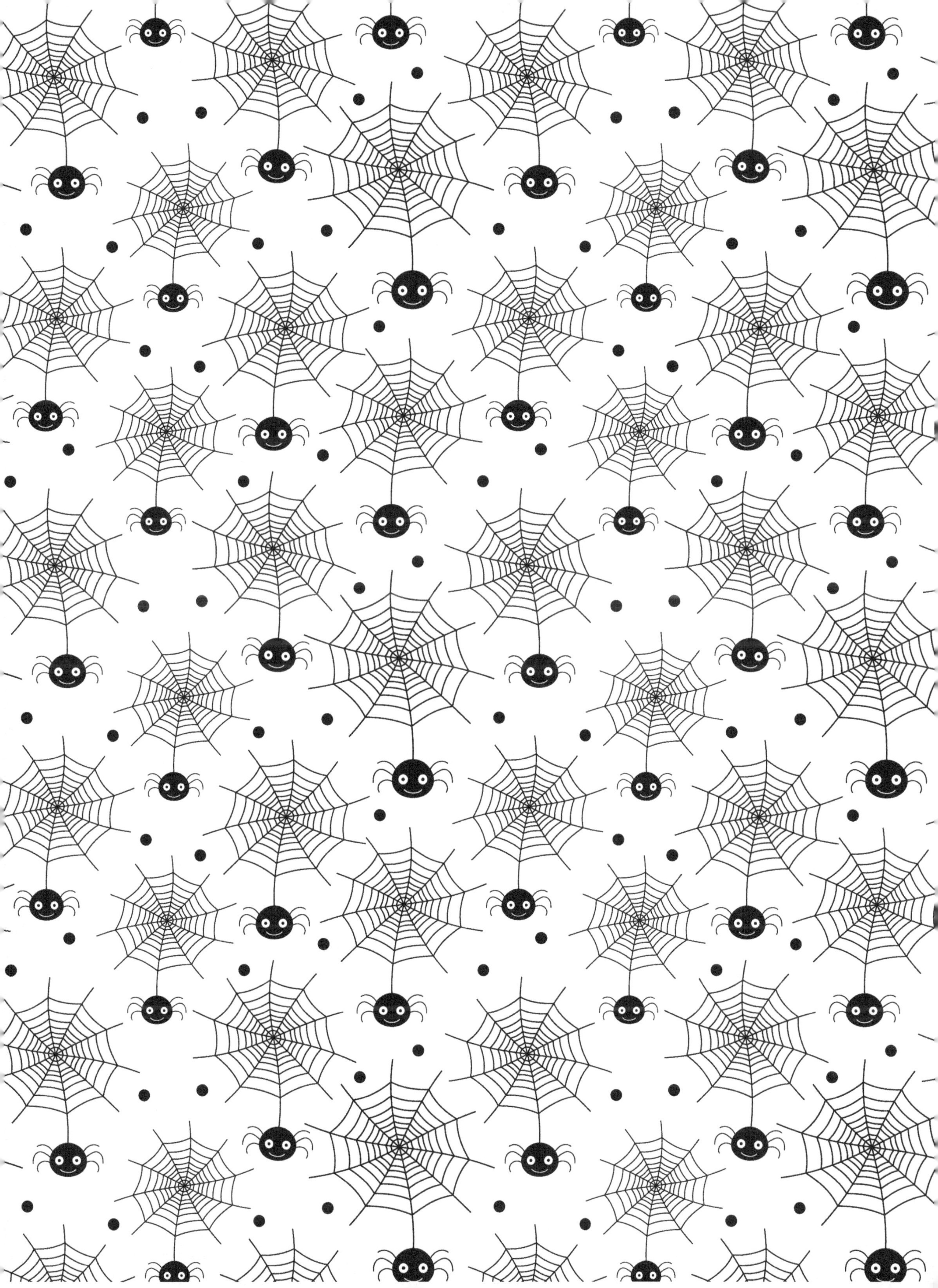

Made in the USA
Coppell, TX
26 October 2019

10492113R00057